SYSTEM VS. CREATOR

system vs. creator

MAKE THE SYSTEM WORK FOR YOU

Meverly Adjhei Benjamin

COPYRIGHT © 2023 MEVERLY ADJHEI BENJAMIN
All rights reserved.

SYSTEM VS. CREATOR
Make the System Work for You

FIRST EDITION

ISBN   978-1-5445-4491-5 *Hardcover*
          978-1-5445-4490-8 *Paperback*
          978-1-5445-4489-2 *Ebook*

Contents

1. THROUGH THE CLAMOR OF LIFE 9
2. WHAT COST PRINCIPLES? 15
3. WHAT GOOD OLD DAYS? 17
4. LIVE TO WORK, OR WORK TO LIVE? 21
5. COURAGE OF OUR CONVICTIONS 25
6. EVALUATION AND DETERMINATION 29
7. TILL DEATH DO US PART—OR TILL SOMEONE BETTER COMES ALONG? 33
8. ALL FOR SHOW? 39
9. IS THERE ANY POINT ANYMORE? 43
10. TOO STRESSED TO SLEEP 51
11. STRESS AND HEALTH 55
12. WHERE DO WE GO FROM HERE? 57
13. THE TOP TEN HAPPIEST PLACES 61
14. IN PURSUIT OF HAPPINESS 67
15. TWENTY-FIRST CENTURY ILLS 79
16. WHAT IS THE ANSWER? 83
17. FREE YOURSELF 87
18. AIM HIGH 91
19. SET YOUR SOUL FREE 95

CHAPTER 1

Through the Clamor of Life

Have you tweeted today?
What did you say?
Has that new car arrived yet
that you couldn't wait to get?
Has your child got the best cell,
and are their mates well jel?
Do you know what really counts?
Or is it just what's trending round about?
Do you want to keep up with the next man,
or do you want to give yourself a life plan?
Are you going to follow like a sheep
or search your soul and dig deep?
Will you find what your true purpose is
or follow what everyone else does?
The thing about being a sheep will be
that market day always comes, you see.
Better to find the way you can thrive

rather than react to envy to keep you alive.
Let them go and get that new car.
Let them travel, no matter how far.
Let them buy the latest and costliest gear.
Just let them go, and have no fear.
If you trust yourself and a higher power,
you'll discover your purpose and your desires will lower.
You will become your own unique success.
You will stand tall and proud, and you'll progress.
Read these words and start today.
Listen and learn from what I say.
I've been there, too, and I've survived.
You can, as well, and stand tall with pride.

—AMANDA THOMAS

You would only have to listen to the news for a few minutes every day to realize that the world we're living in is in a sorry state. Every day, we hear about famine, drought, wars, earthquakes, floods, and acts of such mindless violence that they take our breath away. So how do we live in a world like this, and how do we make sense of life when, for so many people, there is only misery and degradation? Has every generation thought that their time was the worst time, that the future looked bleak, that there was barely any hope for the future?

There have been many words written, over time, about the state of the world we live in, but now, as we look around, words written thousands of years ago in the Bible begin to have an eerily prophetic accuracy about them. Read these two verses from the book of Mark, and then read them again. Does anything sound familiar?

You will hear about wars. You will also hear people talking about future wars. Don't be alarmed. Those things must happen. But the end still isn't here. Nation will fight against nation. Kingdom will fight against Kingdom. There will be earthquakes in many places. People will go hungry. All of those things are the beginning of birth pains (Mark 13:7, 8 ESV).

Another source, Dr. Yuval Noah Harari's book *Sapiens*, is described in this evocative write-up:

> The book *Sapiens* by Dr Yuval Noah Harari takes us on a journey through the whole of human history and shows us how out of six original species of human, hours, Homo Sapiens has been the only one to survive. Through studying palaeontology, biology, anthropology and economics he looks at how our past has influenced the here and now and makes his readers wonder what homo Sapiens and their world will look like in another millennia.
>
> Bold, wide-ranging and provocative, *Sapiens* challenges everything we thought we knew about being human: our thoughts, our actions, our power…and our future.[1]

In my book, I hope that, through a simple, non-expert examination, we can make some sense of the world today and determine if or how we can make any difference to the world tomorrow. I'm sure we are all tired of learned voices telling us what they want us to know, from the causes of crime to

---

1   Yuval Noah Harari, *Sapiens: A Brief History of Humankind* (New York: Vintage, 2015; originally published Penguin Random House, 2011), book blurb, accessed April 17, 2023, https://www.goodreads.com/book/show/23692271-sapiens.

predictions of disaster to global warming. It's time that we as laypeople take control and come to our own conclusions.

If you broach a subject with a hundred people, you'll get a hundred different opinions on it. But the only opinion that really counts in your life is your own. At the end of your life, it will be you who has to answer for what you have done, how you've lived your life, and the legacy you have left behind. I want this book to be an exploration of life in the twenty-first century and how we, as experts in only our own lives, can make sense of what is going on around us. Can we change things? Do we *want* to change things? How can we make those changes? Is this a matter of the system versus the creator? If so, what are the arguments for the system, and what are the arguments for the creator?

Whether you are a Christian, Buddhist, Sikh, Muslim, Hindu, or any other religion, or no religion at all, you will find benefits from following my own quest for some of the answers to the questions that plague us.

Let's start with jobs. Prof. David Graeber, in his book *Bullshit Jobs: A Theory*, gives us this to think about:

> Many of us might wonder if our job did not exist, would it make a difference? Our future was once predicted to be one of just a few hours worked each week and transport to and from that job being by flying car. Of course the pandemic has also thrown a hand grenade into the traditional way of working with many people now being able to work from home rather than from an office space. One book—*Bullshit Jobs* by David Graeber takes a lively look at jobs that appear to be an end in themselves rather than actually offering any productive outcome.[2]

---

[2] David Graeber, *Bullshit Jobs: A Theory* (New York: Simon & Schuster, 2018), 259.

Let's look closer at the kinds of jobs we do and what those jobs are worth to us and our society. We have all heard the saying, "Work to live, rather than live to work," but what does that mean? We have to work, don't we? If we don't work, we don't eat. We have no place to live. We have no status, and we can't bring up children. Is that all true? Someone has to do that job, right? Should we be proud of whatever we do if it is allowing us to provide for our family and keep a roof over our heads?

CHAPTER 2

What Cost Principles?

If you are living hand to mouth, it can be quite difficult to see the bigger picture.

Is there a simpler way? Opportunities accessible to all, no matter their earnings? You would think so—you would hope so—but there is no doubt that choices diminish along with a lack of money. With more people in the UK than ever having to rely on food banks to feed their families, what has gone wrong?

An article in the *Independent* newspaper written by Social Affairs Correspondent May Bulman reported that the delivery of food in response to crisis in the UK increased, and low-income families were the most likely to be in need of this type of referral, along with those who have suffered with debt.[3]

In the current crisis, reliance on food banks is widely publicized, and now, worryingly, it is not just those in disad-

---

3   Quoted in Harriet Agerholm, "Spoof Fundraising Page 'For Katie Hopkins' Legal Fees' Raises Thousands for Food Banks," *Independent*, March 12, 2017, https://www.independent.co.uk/news/uk/home-news/spoof-fundraising-page-katie-hopkins-legal-fees-food-banks-trussel-trust-a7625171.html.

vantaged groups but those who are working who also need to rely on food banks because the money they are earning simply cannot pay for what they need in terms of energy, the price of which has spiraled out of control, as well as their everyday groceries. It seems almost incomprehensible that a country that is among the richest and most influential in the world should have so many people relying on food banks and so many people suffering in this economic crisis. Delays in the benefit system have also contributed to people needing to rely on food bank facilities.

Katie Hopkins, who controversially refused to become Alan Sugar's apprentice when she won the TV show *The Apprentice,* has since then become a general agitator and someone who looks down their nose on most other people. She has previously derided those who rely on food banks, saying that "they are giving free food to dependents who have honed their blagging skills from years on the take."[4] It is hard to imagine that anyone would have such a jaundiced view of a situation that clearly does exist. And that is another concern in today's society: for every situation, no matter how tragic, there will always be a troll who makes it their mission in life to heap misery on misfortune. While there may be people who would abuse the system, there are many more—the majority, in fact—who are victims of circumstance and genuinely need the help that they apply for.

What kind of society thrives on trolling, on making people's lives miserable, on spreading hatred and insults and generally showing a complete lack of empathy or humanity to their fellow man?

---

4   Agerholm, "Spoof Fundraising Page."

CHAPTER 3

What Good Old Days?

Speak to anybody who was brought up in the 1940s, 1950s, and 1960s, and you will hear them say that people in those days were polite, considerate, in harmony, helpful to their neighbors, and willing to help people in need. So what has happened in the subsequent decades to require new laws against cyberbullying or result in losing young people every year to suicide?

Government and law enforcement admit that they are fighting a losing battle against crime committed on the internet. Is this the genie that's been let out of the bottle and can no longer be contained? Has the advent of the internet exposed us all to the many horrors committed by shadowy figures hiding in cyberspace?

There is the good that it has done—and it has done a lot of good: instant information at our fingertips and immediate communication with people all over the world are obvious advantages.

Because of the reach of the internet, children are being bullied, exposed to pornographic material, and generally overwhelmed with age-inappropriate information. What can we mortals do to stem the tide? In the course of this book, we will look at all the problems that face us today that no one seems to have the answers to.

For inspiration, let's turn to the Bible and to other writings that may shed light on the struggle between the system and the creator. For Christians, we are now, in many areas of society, very far from the Bible's teachings. Crime seems to be more violent and more frequent. Is that because we can access more and more information through the internet, and is the information skewing our perception of the world? Maybe it is just that the internet allows us instant and comprehensive access to everything.

There are many questions that we would all like the answers to, but will we ever get them? Who do we even ask to answer them? And if we had the answers, would we like them? Do we need to give up our quest for a bigger house, a new car, the latest designer handbag, or a high-status job? Is that the only way to survive in the twenty-first century? And if we can survive in another way in this world, what is that way? Can we deliver our ideal life ourselves, or do we need governments and other authorities to do it for us? How can we influence what happens in our communities or other countries, and how do we keep the roof above our heads and our children safe from the dangers that are all around?

I hope that you will join me in this journey to explore what can be done and to challenge what "they" say can't be done. Maybe the problem is that we've given up thinking, given up hoping, given up imagining that we can make any difference in the world—or even on our own street. Let's try to take back some power. Let's try to look around us and see what we can change. Let's also try to understand what the consequences of failing to act will be.

It's time we thought about the world in a broader sense. As the oceans fill up with plastic and air becomes unfit to breathe, we cannot abdicate responsibility and hope that our governments and authorities will solve the problems for us. We may not be able to make major changes, but if each one of us asks the right questions and listens and challenges the answers we are given, even the smallest mindful change will be a step in the right direction. Travel with me through this journey of life in the twenty-first century, and ask questions and listen for the answers. Challenge them when you have to, and reclaim your life!

CHAPTER 4

Live to Work, or Work to Live?

The old question, *Should we live to work or work to live?* has never been more relevant than it is in the twenty-first century. In 2017, Paul Schrodt commented that a person who goes to college and gets a degree has a higher earning potential according to statistics produced by the government in the US.[5] But the mega rich, men like Mark Zuckerberg, Bill Gates, or Richard Branson, defy this benchmark by earning their fortunes without the traditional advantage of higher education.

What is the message we are supposed to take from this? Should we just enter a few talent shows or try to get on a reality TV show and not bother with an academic education? If people study hard and progress in their careers, are they happier than the people who don't? Surely, the ones

---

5   Paul Schrodt, "15 Super Successful People Who Never Graduated College," *Money*, November 9, 2017, https://money.com/15-super-successful-people-who-never-graduated-college/.

who have pursued academic study would not be prevented from gaining fame through a reality show or something similar. People who have come to fame through reality TV or talent shows, however, would not be afforded the same chances in reverse if they didn't have a degree to fall back on. And for every person who succeeds in the reality TV/talent show arena, there are thousands who never make it. Should we be concerned that many young people these days, if asked what they would like to be when they grow up, are likely to say they would like to win *Big Brother* or *Britain's Got Talent,* or maybe appear on *Love Island,* instead of giving the traditional answers of *police officer, train driver, astronaut,* or *nurse?* Are their aspirations any less noble than those of the wannabe train drivers of yesteryear?

While I personally think that it is wrong—and even possibly dangerous—to define a person by what academic qualifications they have or don't have, perhaps we are straying too far away from the well-trodden path. Are we allowing young people to aspire to something that is unlikely to happen (or, at best, that they are unlikely to be able to sustain through a working lifetime)? The hard truth of it is that we all have to work to live. We all have bills to pay, and we all want to fulfill our desires in this life. Doing so costs money. No wonder so many parents battle with their children, attempting to point them down the academic route so they can ensure that their children have the means to support themselves when they are adults.

Is it really right to allow people to follow a dream that has virtually no chance of coming true? On the other hand, is it right to squash the dream of someone when we don't know for certain that it *won't* come true? We've seen the different ways some of the world's wealthiest and most successful people either failed or bypassed a traditional college education—and they've done all right for themselves, haven't they?

CHAPTER 5

Courage of Our Convictions

Some time ago, a young Black man was walking through Rotterdam's Central Station. Within the station, a piano had been placed on the main concourse, and the man sat down and started to play. The people hurrying by, all with trains to catch, people to meet, and places to be, stopped in their tracks. When the man stopped playing, thunderous applause rang out around the station. This man was a real talent. His music was beautiful, and his playing was inspired. People had missed their trains, so captivated were they by his playing. A man in a suit approached him.

"Young man, your playing is absolutely beautiful. Are you studying to become a concert pianist? Is that what you want to be?"

The young man smiled at the man and said quietly, "Sir, my greatest desire is to work in a grocery shop. At the moment, I am unemployed, and I don't have the money to go to college."

Over the next few days, the people who were in the station and heard the young men play took to social media. Before long, everyone was talking about him. People would even come to the railway station when they had no train to catch, in the hope that they might be able to hear him playing the piano.

Before long, the young man was presented with the money he needed to go to college. He also got his wish to work in a grocery store part time, alongside pursuing the dream he had never imagined he would be in a position to follow. The day the money was presented to him, the young man cried.

"Where did you learn to play like that?" somebody asked him.

"I learned to play by watching tutorials on YouTube," the young man said.

No one could believe that such talent had come from studying something on YouTube. The point of this story is that we blame the twenty-first century obsession with social media for a lot of the ills of the modern world, but sometimes we forget how much good it can do as well. This young man could never have afforded music lessons, and a great talent would have been lost to the world if he had not been able to find his talent through watching YouTube.

I suppose the moral of this story, and of any other story that cites social media as either a force for good or evil, is that nothing is ever completely as it seems. The dilemma still exists as to whether we should direct young people toward academic pursuits or let them express themselves in the hope that they, too, will be discovered. The odds will stack against being discovered. On programs like *Britain's Got Talent*, we see what ridicule is heaped on those who dare to try and are awful.

On the other side of the argument, if it were not for the pursuit of academic excellence, there would not be doctors whose skill and mastery save lives. No drugs would have been developed and produced to treat our ills. No discoveries would have been made in Egypt's Valley of the Kings, and no fascinating insights would have been gained from those discoveries about life as it was four thousand years ago.

These days, people value success, whether that comes as a huge multimillion-pound mansion or the most expensive car, jewelry, and clothing from the best designers at the highest costs. Magazines and other media foster the cravings for this kind of success. Are they programming us to view these excesses as the most important thing in the world? Are we being encouraged to think that if somebody has attained the dizzying heights of a multimillion-pound mansion, then they must be the most successful, the best role model—in fact, just short of a superhuman?

If these people have attained, through talent or hard work, the wealth most of us could only ever dream of, should we admire them for their achievements over somebody who has won a TV reality show, for instance? Do we even distinguish between these two groups? Are these people defined by what they have rather than who they are? As young people are bombarded with pictures of successful, wealthy, and good-looking people the same age or not much older than they are, how could they not aspire to be like them? It would even appear that negative press about a person who is very rich doesn't make any difference to the way they are viewed. There are many well-documented cases of falls from grace, and often, the worst that those people need fear is a future appearance on *Most Shocking Celebrities*.

So what about people at the bottom of the pile? What about the people who do the menial jobs that no one aspires to do? Those people are invisible in society; but without them, rubbish would not be cleared, roads would not be repaired, litter would remain untouched, and toilets would not be cleaned. There are many thousands of people doing mundane jobs, day in and day out, to make our societies work. They are largely ignored. As we rush about chasing our own rainbows, the orderly in the hospital who clears up after a sick patient goes unrecognized, monetarily or in any other way.

We hear people bemoaning the fact that nurses, needed by us all at some point, are far less valued than footballers earning thousands of pounds a week.

The imbalance in our society is well known, and by and large, we accept it. But take another look at it. Just because someone can kick a football, does it entitle them to eye-watering riches, a compensation so wildly disproportionate to that of a nurse caring for a dying child or comforting a relative during the hardest hours of their life? The people we rely on in society should, if judged by the value of their contribution, be earning top money. After all, if football suddenly disappeared, we would survive. If nurses and medical attention became unavailable, the impact would be far greater. But this is not how we value people in society—not at all.

CHAPTER 6

Evaluation and Determination

So as we live day by day in our society, are we prepared to have our ideas formed by the media? Do we even see those people in society who make it possible for us to live comfortably and in safety?

I believe every person has worth and talent. It may not be a recognizable talent, and it may not be something that people are prepared to pay them thousands of pounds to do, but just as all the different parts of our own bodies need to work together for us to function and live, all people are essential.

It is easy to look at rich, famous, and talented people and say, "Well, I could be just like them if I was given the chance." But even if they have no discernible talents, they have at least had the courage to raise their heads above the parapet and leave themselves open to the criticism and sometimes breathtaking bullying that the same internet that brought them to fame can deliver. Is that admirable?

They say that, in the UK, the public likes nothing better than to build someone up just to knock them down. And that often seems to be the case. Along with the hardline bullying that the internet and social media deliver to those who dare to be different, there are a lot of people who, perhaps out of jealousy, would like nothing better than to see somebody who has risen to success in the media fall flat on their face.

This is not the case, however, with people who have come to fame and acclaim through academic efforts. So this introduces us to another interesting concept. People we can't read or hear enough about are constantly in the public eye for the dress that they're wearing, for the car that they are driving—do we feel we have ownership over them somehow? Why do we feel free to say what we like about them, to criticize them and watch with satisfaction as their bubbles burst?

Let's take the late Professor Stephen Hawking as an example. Here was a man who, against all odds, lived far longer than doctors predicted his disabilities would allow. He had the most rewarding and far-reaching career that turned into film and book opportunities. Because of his academic background, and maybe because of his disability, people like Professor Hawking don't seem to come into anything like the criticism that more mainframe media stars do.

Does that mean that while we feel free to target those in the media who have come by their fame and fortune through reality shows, those who do have an academic background, even if they stray into the realms of media, will not suffer the same fate as those with no academic background? There are many examples of people in the media who also have studied to get where they are. People like super vet Noel Fitzpatrick and some of the great chefs that we see on small screens will rarely be subjected to the same hostility as the Johnny-come-latelys who come to us via reality TV and talent shows. So what does this say about us as a society? Clearly, we all value the services that the most menial workers provide, and clearly, we all admire and are eternally grateful to people in the medical world, from the orderly who wheels patients to the operating theatre to the nurse who looks after them in the ward. So why, in that case, are these groups of people not more highly valued in monetary terms? Why are their academic qualifications and dedication to helping others not granting them the jobs that attract the highest salaries? And what gives us the right to look down our noses at the road sweeper or refuse collector? What is the difference between the refuse collector and the reality TV star? Without essential workers, we would soon know.

In the twenty-first century, the world is getting ever-more complex. Where do we go from here? Is it too late to put the genie back in the bottle? How do we inspire young people to make the most of their talents without being unrealistic in their expectations surrounding instant fame and fortune? How, as a society, do we ensure that everybody has a chance to develop their talents and that nobody is denied the chance to fulfill that dream? We cannot hope for a society that offers everybody exactly what they need. At the same time, academic qualifications don't make a person more valuable than somebody without them. It is a very complex and complicated situation, and if we look back in history, we may find it has never been much different.

What it will take is the will of the government to recognize contribution according to how the loss of that contribution will affect us as a society. Will it ever happen? I fear that it's doubtful. The world will always be unfair to some and will favor others. What I believe we can do as individuals is to question everything. Question government. Question our own beliefs and standards, and question what we are doing in the world to make things better.

It may seem impossible to change the way we live and the values we have, but the first step, I believe, is to have a conversation—at least with ourselves—if we can ever hope to make any difference at all.

CHAPTER 7

Till Death Do Us Part—or Till Someone Better Comes Along?

The Family Research Council has an interesting site. On it, Andreas Kostenberger looks at the next topic that I want to talk about: marriage! In his work, *The Bible's Teaching on Marriage and Family: The Current Cultural Crisis*, he says: "Incredible as it may seem, we can no longer assume that people in our culture understand what the proper definition of 'marriage' and 'the family' is. Not only is this a sad commentary on the impact of same-sex marriage activists on our society, [but] it also shows how the culture's memory of the biblical tradition on which it is largely based is fading fast."[6]

---

6   Andreas J. Köstenberger, *The Bible's Teaching on Marriage and Family* (Washington, DC: Family Research Council, 2011), https://downloads.frc.org/EF/EF11J34.pdf, 1.

He asks us to look at singleness, divorce, and remarriage, according to their biblical definitions.

So first of all, he asks, "Is marriage a contract or a covenant?"

> Today, marriage and the family are regularly viewed as social conventions that can be entered into and severed by the marital partners, at will. As long as a given marriage relationship meets the needs of both individuals involved and is considered advantageous by both sides, the marriage is worth sustaining. If one or both partners decide that they will be better off by breaking up the marriage and entering into a new, better marital union, nothing can legitimately keep them from pursuing their self-interest, self-realization, and self-fulfillment.[7]

He says the cost of divorce takes a toll on the children during the marital separation of their parents. Is their emotional well-being worth losing to safeguard the most cherished principles of our freedom-worshipping, individual rights culture? The answer, he says, seems to be, "If one or both marriage partners want to get out of the marriage, nothing should hold them back."[8]

According to Kostenberger, Scripture teaches that God divinely created marriage and family, not that it is merely a human institution. Kostenberger says that "this means that humans are not free to renegotiate or redefine marriage and the family in any way they choose but that they are called to preserve and respect what has been divinely

---

7 Köstenberger, *Bible's Teaching on Marriage and Family*, 4.

8 Köstenberger, *Bible's Teaching on Marriage and Family*, 4.

instituted. This is in keeping with Jesus' words, uttered when his contemporaries asked him about the permissibility of divorce: 'What therefore God has joined together let no man separate' (Matthew 19:6)."[9] But I wonder—in fact I know—what people who have no religious thoughts at all think about that: nothing!

He says that:

> Marriage is a covenant, a sacred bond between a man and a woman instituted by and publicly entered into before God and normally consummated by sexual intercourse. God's plan for the marriage covenant involves at least the following five vital principles:
>
> 1. The permanence of marriage
> 2. The sacredness of marriage
> 3. The intimacy of marriage
> 4. The mutuality of marriage
> 5. The exclusiveness of marriage [10]

Kostenberger suggests that "there are only two (or possibly three) biblically sanctioned instances of divorce: (1) sexual marital unfaithfulness (i.e., adultery); and (2) the unbelieving spouse's refusal to continue the marriage after the conversion of the other partner. In addition, marital separation (though not necessarily divorce) may be needed in cases of persistent physical spousal abuse."[11]

---

9   Köstenberger, *Bible's Teaching on Marriage and Family*, 5.

10 Köstenberger, *Bible's Teaching on Marriage and Family*, 6.

11 Köstenberger, *Bible's Teaching on Marriage and Family*, 19.

Kostenberger ends his very interesting article with this thought:

> The contemporary culture is in a deep crisis regarding marriage and family today. While the crisis has important political, social, and economic ramifications, in the ultimate analysis only a spiritual return to the biblical foundations will address the root issue of the current crisis. Marriage and the family were God's idea, and as divine institutions they are not open to human renegotiation or revision. As we have seen, the Bible clearly teaches that God instituted marriage as a covenant between one man and one woman, a lifelong union of two partners created in God's image to govern and manage the earth for him. In keeping with his wonderful design, the Creator will normally bless a married couple with children, and it is his good plan that a family made up of a father, a mother, and several children witness to his glory and goodness in a world that has rejected the Creator's plan and has fashioned a variety of God-substitutes to fill the void that can properly be filled only by God himself.[12]

So what relevance in the twenty-first century does this original Biblical description of marriage have? All too often, we see couples married and divorced sometimes in the same year. I'm reminded of another story I heard about the wedding of one of my friends' daughters. Planning for the wedding started two years in advance. The venue was identified, and although it was over budget, it was decided that would be the perfect place. The wedding dress went over budget. The catering went over budget, and the brides-

---

[12] Köstenberger, *Bible's Teaching on Marriage and Family*, 20.

maid's dresses went over budget. In fact, nothing came in on budget at all. The day was spectacular and, after two years of planning, seemed to have been well worth it. Thousands of pounds spent—and the marriage did not even last the year.

CHAPTER 8

All for Show?

With the proliferation of programs on television concentrating on wedding preparations—one even entitled *Bridezillas*—it seems that a wedding these days is more about the trappings than the commitment. In one show, entitled *Don't Tell the Bride*, the groom is given £12,000 to put on a wedding without any input at all from the bride. He chooses the wedding dress, the venue, and everything else to do with the wedding. The aim is clearly to entertain, as the bride weeps over his choice of dress for her—or in one case refuses to go through with the wedding at all, so appalled is she by her groom's choices. The actual message of marriage in this popular program does not appear to be the focus. So what message does this send? That marriage is something to have a laugh about, as some poor unsuspecting bride is dangled over the sea out of a helicopter or subjected to one of many other "fun" things the groom has thought up for his bride's special day? Whenever we do see this type of program, where someone gets ready for the Big Day, the emphasis is always on the actual physical trappings of the day. Plenty of screen time is allotted for the wedding dress and the wedding car, but the hopes and ambitions of the happy couple remain unexamined.

In the world of celebrity, people seem to get married and divorced at regular intervals. It is almost expected—almost as though as their fame grows, they need to change the person sharing their life. How many people actually do believe when they get married that it really will be forever? Do they even listen to themselves as they make their vows? Do they understand that they are entering a contract for life? Even if a person has no religious beliefs and writes their own vows, do they really think as they write them that they are writing or promising something for life? I am not really convinced that people do. And the very fact that so many people get divorced normalizes the process. Even children are possibly less devastated these days when parents split than they would've been long ago because they might now have been the only child in their class whose parents were together.

How much damage are we doing to ourselves and to our children with this "not so much Mr. or Mrs. Right, but more like Mr. or Mrs. Right *Now*" approach?

In an article for *The Guardian*, Rose Hackman reported that she had read that it was men's access to sex that was responsible for the decline of commitment.[13] The article that she read was by sociologist Mark Regnerus and was hardly flattering to the female of the species as he stated, "Why would anybody buy the cow if it's actually being given away?"

---

13 Rose Hackman, "Is Marriage Really on the Decline Because of Men's Cheap Access to Sex?," *The Guardian*, June 11, 2018, https://www.theguardian.com/lifeandstyle/2018/jun/11/is-marriage-really-on-the-decline-because-of-mens-cheap-access-to-sex.

Hackman takes as a fictional example "Tim," who hasn't married at the age of forty. Hackman says that even so, this does not mean Tim definitely will not marry at some time in the future. For Tim, being the right type of partner is as important as finding the correct person to have as his partner. So maybe the message is to wait until later before you tie the knot.

CHAPTER 9

Is There Any Point Anymore?

If we do wait to get married until we are older and know better what we want, will that solve the problem? Are the old values of "till death do us part" relevant anymore in the twenty-first century? Should we be looking at shorter contractual periods that can be renewed? Does it even matter that marriages end in divorce, when so many people live together without any formalities at all?

What about the children who are brought up in an ever-changing parental landscape? How does this affect their growth, their grounding, and their sense of self? Does having a stepparent as well as parents better broaden horizons? I suppose the answer will be in the relationships that exist between the adults in a child's life. Arguably, more damage will be done to children if they live with parents who are constantly battling and are staying together "for the children." But it can be very difficult to maintain equilibrium within the adults of a broken relationship, especially if one feels cheated or harmed by a spouse who has strayed. In these cases, anger, resentment, and bitterness will not offer an atmosphere that a child can thrive in.

Do adults think about the effect that breaking up with their child's other parent will have on that child? Are they only considering what makes them happy and fulfilled?

People seem to show little thought to repairing a relationship that has hit a bump in the road. They're so quick to throw in the towel; in fact, they are encouraged to do so by the media. On any weekday morning, viewers in the UK can tune in to the Jeremy Kyle show and watch people in the most dysfunctional relationships hurling abuse and the most hateful comments at each other—while on the screen behind them, a film of a child (often the subject of a paternity test) is shown. I have seen episodes of this show where there have been no less than four potential fathers. Clearly, we can't go back to the days when sex before marriage was very taboo, nor should we, but I do believe people need to get to know each other in all respects before they get married.

The early teachings on marriage that we got initially from the Bible advocate one man and one woman bringing up children together. There are clearly a lot of advantages to this way of producing and nurturing a family. People in their fifties and sixties will talk warmly of the fact that they lived in a time when divorce was not at all common and they clearly value that they were brought up by a mother and father in a traditional family. Nowadays, a marriage can be between people of the same sex as well as the opposite sexes. Many welcome this more inclusive way of producing a family. They argue that if the child is raised with love, who does the raising is largely immaterial. I suppose time will tell whether this shift in tradition, or the traditional family, is for better or worse.

For many years, a civil partnership was the closest same-same couples could get to a traditional marriage. Now, marriage is permitted between same-sex couples in exactly the same way as it is for heterosexual couples. But this change did not come about without a considerable fight and struggle. This is proof that people do still value the institution of marriage and are prepared to fight hard for the right to enter into it.

But whose responsibility is it, ultimately, to make people aware of the sanctity of marriage and how it should look? Is it the church's responsibility? Is it the state's responsibility? Is it society's values that need to be put under a microscope and redefined?

When people make their vows, how seriously do they take them? With marriages collapsing at a rate of almost one in two, how confident can anybody be that their marriage will stand the test of time? Or are they prepared for forever just for the moment, until the pressure of society or their own desire to make and keep themselves happy takes over?

I am a believer in marriage, although I respect other people's right to live in whatever way they like. I am also a believer in giving children an upbringing that is as carefree and happy as it possibly can be. That is why I believe that for the sake of our children, we need to make different choices, or to postpone having a child until we feel we are in a relationship that will last.

To end with, here are a collection of inspirational, wise, and humorous old marriage quotes, sayings, and proverbs, collected over the years from a variety of sources by wiseoldsayings.com.[14]

"To keep your marriage brimming, with love in the loving cup, whenever you're wrong admit it; whenever you're right shut up."

—OGDEN NASH

"Marriage is an alliance entered into by a man who can't sleep with the window shut, and a woman who can't sleep with the window open."

—GEORGE BERNARD SHAW

"One advantage of marriage is that, when you fall out of love with him or he falls out of love with you, it keeps you together until you fall in again."

—JUDITH VIORST

"A successful marriage requires falling in love many times, always with the same person."

—MIGNON MCLAUGHLIN

"After marriage, husband and wife become two sides of a coin; they just can't face each other, but still they stay together."

—HERMANT JOSHI

"The secret of a happy marriage remains a secret."

—HENNY YOUNGMAN

---

14 "Marriage Sayings and Quotes," Wise Sayings, accessed April 17, 2023, https://www.wisesayings.com/marriage-quotes.

"A great marriage is not when the perfect couple comes together. It is when an imperfect couple learns to enjoy their differences."

—DAVE MEURER

"Many marriages would be better if the husband and the wife understood that they are on the same side."

—ZIG ZIGLAR

"A long marriage is two people trying to dance a duet and two solos at the same time."

—ANNE TAYLOR FLEMING

"The great secret of successful marriage is to treat all disasters as incidents and none of the incidents as disasters."

—HAROLD GEORGE NICOLSON

"Chains do not hold a marriage together. It is threads, hundreds of tiny threads, which sew people together through the years."

—SIMONE SIGNORET

"A good marriage is the union of two good forgivers."

—RUTH BELL GRAHAM

"Marriage, ultimately, is the practice of becoming passionate friends."

—HARVILLE HENDRIX

"Marriage, like a submarine, is only safe if you get all the way inside."

—FRANK PITTMAN

"A good marriage is a contest of generosity."

—DIANE SAWYER

"Marriages are like fingerprints; each one is different and each one is beautiful."

—MAGGIE REYES

"The difference between an ordinary marriage and an extraordinary marriage is in giving just a little extra every day, as often as possible, for as long as we both shall live."

—FAWN WEAVER

"The greatest marriages are built on teamwork, mutual respect, a healthy dose of admiration, and a never-ending portion of love and grace."

—FAWN WEAVER

"A long-lasting marriage is built by two people who believe in—and live by—the solemn promise they made."

—DARLENE SCHACHT

"A great marriage isn't something that just happens; it's something that must be created."

—FAWN WEAVER

"Marriage is like watching the colour of leaves in the fall; ever changing and more stunningly beautiful with each passing day."

—FAWN WEAVER

"In marriage, each partner is to be an encourager rather than a critic, a forgiver rather than a collector of hurts, an enabler rather than a reformer."

—H. NORMAN WRIGHT

"What counts in making a happy marriage is not so much how compatible you are, but how you deal with incompatibility."

—LEO TOLSTOY

"Marriage is more than finding the right person. It is being the right person."

—UNKNOWN

CHAPTER 10

Too Stressed to Sleep

Are there more pressures, more expectations on us, more sleepless nights? You bet there are!

In the past century, the negativity in life has increased because we have become more addicted to ambition, success, fame, and money. We don't know where to stop. The hunger to achieve more and more is eating us from the inside. We are also becoming selfish and self-centered. We put ourselves before our family and friends—before anything. Young people don't listen to their parents, and they lie to them with ease when they need to. The culture of the nuclear family is missing these days among many fractured and broken families. As a result, parents are forced to live alone in their old age, when the support from their children is needed the most, and children don't get the amount of love and care that they used to get in the traditional larger family group.

Our society is highly influenced by the "What will people say?" mindset. This societal pressure forces expectations on children. Often, they are not able to handle the burden of expectations. As a consequence, they make the wrong decisions.

Then there are the almost-normalized bad habits like drinking, smoking, and narcotics use at an early age that claim teenagers and are hard to detach from. The "peer pressure" and the "cool culture" are stealing kids' innocence.

We are accustomed to this vicious circle of routine and a monotonous life. But humans are meant to be adventurous by definition. It follows, then, that this "same thing every day" routine brings boredom into our lives—and many of us struggle to deal with it, feeling unhappy and on edge without even knowing why.

I think that this interpretation of modern ills hits the nail on the head. There is a modern acronym, FOMO, that stands for "fear of missing out." Maybe that is what is wrong with us: we are so afraid of missing out on something that we cannot leave our phones alone. The more we look at them, the more invested we get.

I was walking past a park the other day and saw a couple of mothers walking their babies in prams. It could have been a timeless picture, mother walking baby in the park—except that these mothers, rather than talking to their babies about the trees and the birds, were tapping away on their phones with one hand while pushing the baby or toddler along with the other. There was no interaction. And that, I think, is part of the problem. Those little things that we used to enjoy, like interaction with our mothers as we were pushed along the street or through the park, might be lost in the mists of time, and their value may not be realized. There is a generation of children now growing up without that early interaction, who are pacified not with soft words from mum but with an electronic device to entertain them with cartoons or anything that will keep them quiet. No wonder, then, that we grow up to be stressed and sleep deprived. Technology is taking over our lives. Now, I am not saying that we should go back to the pre-tech days—we couldn't if we wanted to—but maybe, just maybe, we need tech to work for us in our lives rather than being controlled by alerts emitted every waking hour from our phones and other devices.

By the time we grow up and start work, things are even rougher. The stress of surviving childhood and the threat of social media trolling and judgment online makes way for the world of work.

In 2019, Brigette Hyacinth wrote about what happens when a boss becomes a dictator, routinely embarrassing or overruling or even firing employees who don't toe the line.[15] This is a situation that results in a toxic workplace. This toxicity comes not just from the behavior of the employer but also from the fact that the workforce is constantly in fear. It can even cause people to betray other people just to curry favor with their boss. This type of environment could never hope to be fully productive.

Here are the signs that you are working in a toxic workplace:

1. The function of the organization is not in alignment with the core values of the company.
2. No feedback is given, as people are afraid to speak out and any suggestions are ignored.

---

15 Brigette Hyacinth, "Toxic Work Cultures Make Best Employees Quit," LinkedIn, June 11, 2019, https://www.linkedin.com/pulse/toxic-work-cultures-make-best-employees-quit-brigette-hyacinth/.

3. There is bullying and blatant favoritism
4. Micromanagement is stifling employees.
5. The blame game is rife, with management picking on employees.
6. Levels of absenteeism due to sickness are high.
7. Long hours are seen as a badge of honor.
8. There is no line of communication between employees and their managers.
9. An excessive clique and gossiping atmosphere prevails.
10. Staff turnover is high.[16]

---

16 Hyacinth, "Toxic Work Cultures."

CHAPTER 11

Stress and Health

Stress is toxic, and it can negatively affect the body in many ways. A 2015 BBC article discusses the link between depression and heart failure.[17] The work that they carried out for this study suggested that a cardiology patient who was also suffering from depression had a much higher chance of dying from their cardiac disease within a year of diagnosis. They presented their findings to the European Society of Cardiology and suggested that patients who were suffering from depression as well as cardiac disease should consult their GP or get counseling to address their depression.

A study like this would have been unthinkable years ago—a link between heart disease and depression? Well, we may think that it would be natural for someone who was ill to be depressed, but linking depression to the onset of heart disease was not something people were ready to think about.

---

[17] "Heart Failure Victims Require Depression Counselling," BBC News, May 23, 2015, https://www.bbc.com/news/health-32846280.

Living in the twenty-first century is full of stresses and pressure, and the environment that we live and work in can seem, at times, increasingly toxic. Older people look back longingly to the days when life was not so complicated, and people seemed to have more time for each other. But if you are growing up in the twenty-first century, there is no point in looking backward because, somehow, we need to make a future for ourselves.

CHAPTER 12

Where Do We Go from Here?

"We are all living together on a single planet, which is threatened by our own actions. And if you don't have some kind of global cooperation, nationalism is just not on the right level to tackle the problems, whether it's climate change or whether it's technological disruption."

—YUVAL NOAH HARARI

This quote from Yuval Harare sums up the message that we all need to be hearing loud and clear in the twenty-first century. Not a day goes by when we don't hear about the effect of global warming on our planet and on our everyday lives. Somehow, as we travel the world or even our own locality, we need to be able to make sense of the world around us and how it affects us. We need to feel hope for our children and the world that they will inherit. There will be people who deny global warming even exists, and there will be people who deny that anything is wrong at all with the way we live. For most of us, however, a deep concern and worry can knock us off track and make us abandon or postpone the dreams we have as pressure bears down on us.

But whatever the obstacles, whatever the pressure, whatever the sorrow, whatever the pain, we have to keep going. We have to hold on to the dreams that we have and make them come true.

Maybe we need to take a step back from our lives and have a look at that big picture again. Maybe the obstacles we face seem bigger than they actually are. If so, we need to regroup, reassess, and redirect our efforts so that we can go where we need to go and do what we need to do to make our future what we want it to be.

For some people, religion will help. I am one of those people, and my faith has helped me through the many traumas I have faced in my life. But I don't only want to speak to people who have faith in God; even faith in just yourself will go a long way in helping you realize your dreams.

There can come a time in everybody's life when it might seem barely worth living. Bereavement, losing a job, or the threat of homelessness, illness, or even prison...all these things can lead to such hopelessness that we just feel it's not worth trying anymore. But for every problem—no matter how complex or overwhelming that problem might be—there will be a solution, an answer, and a way forward.

Whatever helps you through dark days—be it your family, your faith, hope for the future that you had almost allowed to be buried under a mountain of despair—hold on to that, and nurture it like a tiny plant. If given enough care and attention, one day it will grow to be a mighty oak tree. Let the oak tree of your ambition and dreams for the future grow. It won't grow overnight, and you will need to do it carefully to ensure that it keeps growing and thriving.

We have been conditioned in the twenty-first century to expect instant answers to everything and instant gratification of whatever our needs are. Maybe this is part of the discontent that people feel when things just don't happen fast enough and they are left frustrated at the perceived lack of progress being made.

The little oak tree that is the beginning of your journey to success and happiness will grow, but it will grow slowly. We have to be patient as we wait for our hopes and dreams to materialize. Just like a hard frost can damage a young plant, negativity and depression can threaten to derail our efforts and even kill our ambition and our hopes. As part of my tending to the tender shoots of my own dreams, I use prayer, and I find great comfort and inspiration in it. But even without faith in God, it's still possible to believe in yourself and to motivate yourself to get where you want to be. Worthy goals are worth the effort you put in and the sacrifices you make to achieve what you set out to achieve.

With concerns over everything from the planet we live on and its sustainability to the health risks that our busy daily lives impose on us, no wonder so many are living with debilitating stress. People are also worried that their children will become prey to evils and bad influences that, a few decades ago and without the internet, would not have been possible. The questions of how we can keep our planet a viable place to live, how we can make a success of our working life, and how we keep our children safe are headaches that most people have in common.

Never give up, and never feel that life is hopeless. Even in the darkest day, look for a little sliver of light, and that will be your starting point. Just like the oak tree, you can grow slowly but surely—and if you tend to your growth carefully, there will be nothing that you cannot achieve.

Whatever spurs you on, whatever makes you want to hold on even when things look bleak, hold on to it—and make sure that every day you find something to be thankful for and some tiny way in which the situation you find yourself in has improved. Keeping this up will lead you slowly but surely to where you want to be. And when you get there, just imagine the delight and the pride you will feel for having reached your goal.

CHAPTER 13

The Top Ten Happiest Places

A *World Happiness Report* measured housing, diversity, environment, well-being and political stability.[18] In the latest calculations, Finland has come out on top for the country that has the happiest people. Here is the rundown of the happiest countries. In 2019, before COVID, it ranked countries as follows:

1. Finland
2. Denmark
3. Norway
4. Iceland
5. Netherlands
6. Switzerland

---

18   John F. Helliwell, Richard Layard, and Jeffrey D. Sachs, *World Happiness Report 2019* (New York: Sustainable Development Solutions Network, 2019), 27, https://s3.amazonaws.com/happiness-report/2019/WHR19.pdf.

7. Sweden
8. New Zealand
9. Canada
10. Austria
11. Australia[19]

Finland's prize of first place isn't surprising, given that it is the home of Santa Claus and the Northern Lights. But there must be more to it than that, as this country has scooped the title of the happiest place to live for the second year running. Hot on its heels are Norway, Denmark, Iceland, and the Netherlands. Is it a coincidence that all the top countries have colder climates? In fact, the national sport of Finland is ice swimming. So does cold equal happy? And where does that leave our perception that retiring to a hot country will make us happier?

Some of the other things that go toward making a country the place that has the happiest people are freedom, healthy life expectancy, trust, generosity, and social support. The countries that rank in the ten top spots of the "Happiness Survey" all have these characteristics in abundance. However, the "happiness" quotient goes beyond those native to the countries. The study found that immigrants coming to live in Finland also came out top in the happiest immigrants in the world. But this feeling of security, safety, and well-being does come at a cost. Taxes are high in Finland. However, its citizens trust the government, and it seems that the people living in Finland genuinely care about each other and are embodying the instruction to "love thy neighbor." That, it seems, is just the kind of

---

[19] Helliwell, Layard, and Sachs, *World Happiness Report 2019*, 29.

atmosphere that people want and need to live in for their happiness.

So maybe we need to remember that simple old biblical instruction to "love thy neighbor"? You will often hear people in their fifties and sixties recalling that when they were children, everybody had time for each other. Neighbors looked out for neighbors and most people up and down the street knew each other.

So let's look at one of those "happy countries" and some of the top reasons Australians, and those who have moved to Australia, have a high ranking for happiness. The first thing is probably work-life balance. A recent survey conducted by the OECD Australia (Organisation for Economic Cooperation and Development) cites the outdoor lifestyle and competitive salaries.[20] Their emphasis on a true balance means that the quality of life offered in Australia is second to none. Although it's true that Australians understand the importance of financial security and work, they are also very aware of the time they need to devote to their family and friends, to their hobbies, and to keeping themselves fit. The climate and the landscapes can be a great encouragement to living a more active outdoor lifestyle and a healthier life overall—and that is a big factor in a happiness quotient.

Low employment rates and a cosmopolitan culture also make this a country in which residents are happy. So does its education system that is the envy of the world.

A comfortable climate to live in is another big factor in Australians' satisfaction and happiness. It is one of the driest continents on the earth, so it is unlikely that rain will often

---

20 "Australia," OECD Better Life Index, accessed August 14, 2023, https://www.oecdbetterlifeindex.org/countries/australia/.

spoil outdoor plans. Health services and life expectancy are also extremely good in Australia, adding to the contentment of those living there.

New Zealand always ranks highly in happiness scores as well and is a very resilient country. Happiness in New Zealand is derived from a feeling of having free choice and full social connection opportunities, as well as pulling together in hard times. Of course the scenery is wonderful, but the quality of life of a New Zealander is also influenced by having a high degree of social support. The education system in New Zealand is excellent, as is the health system. The very forward-thinking former Prime Minister Jacinda Ahern, who guided her country so well through the COVID-19 pandemic, was also the first premier in the world to introduce a well-being budget that was allocated to projects that dealt with digital transformation, climate change, health and housing, social exclusion, and domestic violence.

Canadian citizens owe their sense of contentment and happiness to the fact that they are reportedly generally satisfied with their day-to-day lives. In Canada, happiness comes from having very good prospects for income, excellent health services, social safety, and a general acceptance of all races and creeds. Canadian citizens also measure their happiness based on the fact that they tend to have strong family ties. Friends and coworkers are also part of the happiness quotient. The stunning scenery of the country and good housing stock also have a big bearing on how happy the Canadian population feels.

We should not get carried away in thinking that these ten happiest countries are a complete utopia. The fact that they rank high for happiness does not mean that any of these countries are immune to trauma or violence. Indeed, number eight on the list, New Zealand, recently experienced a horrific and deadly attack on worshippers in a mosque in which many people lost their lives. What we do notice, and a fact that perhaps sets New Zealand apart, is how her people responded to this attack.

In the face of such horror stands the resilience and the ability of the people to deal with the aftermath. After the recent attack on the mosque, and after a 2011 earthquake struck Christchurch, people came together, rallied, and helped each other. It was a community at work. People were "loving their neighbors."

If we look at another large country, the United States, we see that its ranking in the measure of happiness has dropped from eighteenth to nineteenth—and, in fact, it now ranks five spots lower than it did in the 2019 *World Happiness Report*.[21] While it ranks in the top ten for income, it is nowhere near the top ten in the measure of an overall "happy" country. Instead, it ranks thirty-seventh for the social support offered, a worrying forty-second for corruption, and a woeful sixty-first place for a feeling of freedom.

Jeffrey Sachs, the director of the Sustainable Development Solutions Network, and Jean. M. Twenge, psychologist and author of *iGen*, September 7, 2019, say that part of the reason the US does not rank higher is the epidemic of addiction and depression in the country.[22] Twenge points a finger at social media as a cause for depression in more girls than boys. Sachs also points out that addiction is no longer confined to the traditional areas of drink and drugs but now includes things like gambling and addiction to digital media.

---

21 Helliwell, Layard, and Sachs, *World Happiness Report 2019*, 29.
22 Helliwell, Layard, and Sachs, *World Happiness Report 2019*, 127.

Compulsively pursuing substance abuse and other addictive behaviors is at the root of a lot of severe unhappiness. Rather than strengthening social connections, social media has become everyday currency in communication, especially among the young.

Interestingly, none of the so-called superpowers appear on the top ten for happiness. The United Kingdom is in fifteenth place, although that did represent a three-point rise from eighteenth place from the year before. Way down the list are countries like Japan in spot fifty-eight, Russia in sixty-eight, and China in ninety-three.

The report has said that the people of South Sudan are the unhappiest people, and the people of the Central African Republic, Afghanistan, Tanzania, and Rwanda are not happy either—unsurprising, since most have had major problems with war and other unrest.[23]

---

23 Helliwell, Layard, and Sachs, *World Happiness Report 2019*, 29.

CHAPTER 14

In Pursuit of Happiness

If you ask someone who is depressed or unhappy what they would like most, they might very likely say they would love to be happy again, even for just a little while.

In the last chapter, we dealt with the stresses and strains that we are under in the twenty-first century, and in this chapter, I want to deal with what makes us happy. For that, I went first to the Statistical Appendix for Chapter 2 of the 2019 *World Happiness Report* by John F. Helliwell, Haifang Huang, and Shun Wang.[24]

They used statistics of healthy life expectancies at birth based on the data produced by the World Health Organization's Global Health Observatory data repository.

They used stats for social support (having someone to count on in times of trouble), asking the question, "If you

---

24 John F. Helliwell, Haifang Huang, and Shun Wang, "Statistical Appendix 1 for Chapter 2 of World Happiness Report 2019," March 7, 2019, 3, https://s3.amazonaws.com/happiness-report/2019/WHR19_Ch2A_Appendix1.pdf.

were in trouble, do you have relatives or friends you can count on to help you whenever you need them, or not?"

The next question was, "Are you satisfied or dissatisfied with your freedom to choose what you do with your life?"

Generosity was next, with this question: "Have you donated money to a charity in the past month?"

Where the perception of corruption was concerned, the questions asked were: "Is corruption widespread throughout the government or not?" and "Is corruption widespread within businesses or not?"[25]

The happiness study defined positive affect as the average of three positive affect measures: happiness, laughter, and enjoyment. The study authors asked participants:

> "Did you experience the following feelings during A LOT OF THE DAY yesterday? How about Happiness?" "Did you smile or laugh a lot yesterday?" "Did you experience the following feelings during A LOT OF THE DAY yesterday? How about Enjoyment?"[26]

Dealing with negative affect, the study defined that as the average of three negative affect measures: worry, sadness, and anger. The study authors sought responses to these questions:

> "Did you experience the following feelings during A LOT OF THE DAY yesterday? How about worry?" "Did you experience the following feelings during A LOT OF THE DAY yesterday?

---

25 Helliwell, Layard, and Sachs, *World Happiness Report 2019*, 25.

26 Helliwell, Huang, and Wang, "Statistical Appendix 1," 3.

How about sadness?" "Did you experience the following feelings during A LOT OF THE DAY yesterday? How about anger?"[27]

To calculate income and the effect that had on happiness scores, the people in the survey were asked to report their household income in local currency.

The results of this scientific approach varied widely from place to place and country to country.

In a sermon in Westminster Abbey, London, on March 20, 1925, Frederick Lewis Donaldson said that the Seven Social Sins are:

1. Wealth without work
2. Pleasure without conscience
3. Knowledge without character
4. Commerce without morality
5. Science without humanity
6. Worship without sacrifice
7. Politics without principle[28]

WEALTH WITHOUT WORK

Getting money for doing nothing is not ideal for our happiness. As human beings, we respond with pride, a sense of achievement, and happiness when we work hard and see the reward for our labors.

---

27 Helliwell, Huang, and Wang, "Statistical Appendix 1," 3.

28 Charles Hoffacker, sermon, Westminster Abbey, London, March 20, 1925, quoted in Charles Hoffacker, "The Anglican Origin of the Seven Social Sins," The Living Church, December 1, 2022, https://livingchurch.org/2022/12/01/the-anglican-origin-of-the-seven-social-sins/.

PLEASURE WITHOUT CONSCIENCE

To feel pleasure, we need to know that what makes us happy is not at the expense or because of the suffering of others. Stealing is an example of obtaining what we want without paying for it, although it is clearly the wrong thing to do. We need a conscience to inform us about what gives us pleasure.

KNOWLEDGE WITHOUT CHARACTER

Knowledge is a good thing, but using what we know irresponsibly and without thought for others is not the road to happiness for us or for other people.

COMMERCE WITHOUT MORALITY

Commerce and big business make the world go round, but practicing business without morality can land us in deep water, as we have seen through the collapse of seemingly unsinkable financial institutions through greed and mismanagement. Morality should be the first requirement for anyone in power in commercial superpowers.

SCIENCE WITHOUT HUMANITY

We all have a lot to thank science for, and many diseases that killed our ancestors in the hundreds of thousands have now been eradicated. But there are other aspects of scientific research and advancement that bring with them questions on the wisdom of the advances they offer. Premature babies are one area I can think of where the wisdom of saving very early babies can be questioned. Doing so often leaves them and their families with a lifelong commitment to dealing with the disabilities that being born very much too early can bring. Just because you can, should you?

WORSHIP WITHOUT SACRIFICE

It is all very well to pay lip service to our God and our religion and call ourselves devout followers of that religion—but without making sacrifices of our time and effort, can we really call ourselves devout? Can we really be happy with the effort we put into our religion?

POLITICS WITHOUT PRINCIPLE

There have been many examples of what happens when people in power have no principles, and it normally doesn't end well. In this case, however, leaders may be happy with how they are, but those they govern certainly will not be.

A good contribution to our debate comes from Steve Spring's article "Happiness. What Is It and Why Does It Matter to You?"[29]

In his article, Spring says that there are some questions around happiness that all of us may think of from time to time. One interesting point that Spring makes, which I totally agree with, is that human beings will always have some sadness in their life. The difference is that if you are generally and naturally an optimistic and happy person, you will bounce back quicker than someone who has a more glass-half-empty approach to life. That made me wonder

---

29 Steve Spring, "Happiness. What Is It and Why Does It Matter to You?," *Be Yourself*, Medium, June 22, 2018, https://medium.com/life-tips/happiness-what-is-it-and-why-does-it-matter-to-you-2d5db02e62a9.

about the role that genetics has to play in whether we are the half-full or half-empty type of person. In fact, Spring attributes at least half of our ability to be a happy person to our genetics. The other half of our potential to be happy is down to the circumstances we meet through our lives.

HAVING A LOT OF MONEY DOES NOT EQUAL HAPPINESS

No one would argue that suffering severe poverty and deprivation would make it quite difficult to be carefree and happy. The interesting thing is, however, that there is a point that you can arrive at in terms of wealth where accumulating any more Riches will make little or no difference to your happiness. In times gone by, it was always assumed that the more money you had, the happier you would be. Benjamin Franklin famously said that it was not money that would make a man happy, and it never had been. He pointed out that there is nothing in the actual nature of money that can actually, practically produce happiness. In fact, he observed that the more money somebody has, the more, typically, they want.

Recent research by psychologists from Purdue University and the University of Virginia have confirmed findings of studies by Daniel Kahneman that concluded that income beyond $75,000 per year did not increase people's happiness.[30]

Purdue University and the University of Virginia carried out an analysis of a Gallup poll with data that had

---

[30] Daniel Kahneman and Angus Deaton, "High Income Improves Evaluation of Life but Not Emotional Well-Being," *Psychological and Cognitive Sciences* 107, no. 38 (September 2010): 16489-16493, https://doi.org/10.1073/pnas.101149210.

been gathered from 164 countries and 1.7 million people. They cross-referenced life satisfaction with the amount of money they had and their earnings. Although there was a wide variety of living standards and costs of living across the countries that were surveyed, the researchers came to the conclusion that the ideal income for any individual would be around $95,000 a year, and between $60,000 and $75,000 a year for them to enjoy a sense of emotional well-being.[31]

The interesting conclusion of both studies is that, up to a certain point, money does improve our feeling of happiness. That number could be lower or higher depending on which country we live in—but for the United States, the figure was $75,000.

When you look at improvement in day-to-day feeling of happiness, however, money will deliver a diminishing return. In some cases, the researchers even found that as money increased, happiness decreased.

HAPPINESS IS A JOURNEY, NOT A DESTINATION

If you speak to anyone today, you will most likely find that they look at happiness as something they remember from their past or something they're looking forward to in their future. Many people will spend a lot of time harping on about the past or talking endlessly about what they're going to achieve sometime in the future. In other words, they are looking at their happiness as a destination rather than a journey.

---

[31] Andrew T. Jebb et al., "Happiness, Income Satiation and Turning Points Around the World," *Nature Human Behavior* 2 (2018): 33–38, https://doi.org/10.1038/s41562-017-0277-0.

It is very easy to forget that we're living in the here and now and that to not concentrate on being happy in the present is to waste many days, months, and even years in pursuit of something that might or might not happen in the future.

Never forget that you are living in the present.

"Happiness is a direction, not a place."

— SYDNEY J. HARRIS

People would be wise to recognize their happiness as a journey and not only as a destination.

No future achievement is likely to bring extreme happiness.

There is no amount of money that can buy happiness.

There is no relationship that can guarantee you will be happy.

We need to teach ourselves to enjoy life in the present moment.

"Happiness is not a station you arrive at, but a manner of travelling."

—MARGARET LEE RUNBECK.

You might arrive at the destination of your dreams but have no memory of the journey that you took to get there. It is a wise person who learns to enjoy the journey while they look forward to reaching the destination.

WHAT EXACTLY IS HAPPINESS?

Good question!

The true meaning of happiness and what can bring us that elusive feeling has been the subject of debate for millennia. The ancient Greeks thought that they had the equation for perfect happiness: *hedonia*, which means pleasure, and *eudaimonia*, which means purpose or meaning. Since that time, psychologists have added something to the definition that the Greeks attached to happiness: engagement, also referred to as flow.

Spring notes that in *Authentic Happiness*, published in 2002, author Martin Seligman proposed that there were three specific orientations to happiness (in other words, three types of happiness): engagement, pleasure, and meaning.[32] Psychologists have coined an overall scientific term to describe happiness. It is called *subjective well-being*, a combination of engagement, meaning, and pleasure. These are qualities that they can actually identify and measure.

In her 2007 book *The Hows of Happiness*, Sonja Lyubomirsky defines a person who is happy as somebody who often feels joy, positive well-being, and contentment in combination with a sense that their life is good, worthwhile, and meaningful.[33]

SO WHAT DOES ALL THIS INFORMATION MEAN TO YOU PERSONALLY?

How happy you are is a mixture of different things, such as how satisfied you are with how your life is going; how good you feel day to day; and how much you engage with your friends, family, and work colleagues.

Interestingly, there is strong evidence suggesting that when people focus on being happy, they might actually

---

[32] Martin E. P. Seligman, *Authentic Happiness: Using the New Positive Psychology to Realize Your Potential for Lasting Fulfillment* (New York: Atria, 2002).

[33] Sonja Lyubomirsky, *The How of Happiness: A New Approach to Getting the Life You Want* (New York: Penguin, 2007).

achieve the opposite for themselves. Iris Mauss found in her study that people who actively and aggressively pursue being happy can actually experience a reduction in how happy they feel.[34] It seems that in the end, it's not trying to make yourself happy that is important, but rather enjoying life in a relaxed way and with the people you feel happiest with.

In conclusion, being happy does not mean constantly feeling pleasure. Being happy does not mean having great wealth. Happiness is not even a destination that you can plot a course for.

Happiness is actually having meaning in your life and satisfaction in living it, as well as feeling emotions that are positive and being able to connect in a positive way with other people. Happiness is more about purpose and meaning than it is about feeling joyous every minute of every day.[35]

Definite food for thought! I agree with what Steve Spring wrote in this provocative article.

As I said at the beginning of this chapter, someone who is down or depressed would give a lot for that feeling of happiness that comes with being free in your mind to enjoy whatever it is you are doing, with no restraint.

I have my faith to help me find happiness. I trust in something greater than myself to guide me and to care for me, help me through the bad times, and show me that there are always better times around the corner. I think we can learn a lot from what Steve Spring says about allowing our-

---

[34] Iris B. Mauss et al., "The Pursuit of Happiness Can Be Lonely," *Emotion* 12, no. 5 (2012): 908–912, https://doi.org/10.1037/a0025299.

[35] Spring, "Happiness."

selves to enjoy life, to park our cares and woes for a while, and to learn to be happy with even the smallest things in our lives. In my case, just a smile from my son can make me happy and fill my heart with joy. It costs nothing but gives much more than happiness: it gives real joy!

Happiness seems to be completely out of reach to some people and a distant dream to others. But maybe they are aiming too high. Maybe we are all missing the tiny things, like a beautiful sunrise or a child's smile—things that are free for us to enjoy and appreciate. Maybe we really are expecting too much.

Let's take a step back in this hectic world and see what is in front of our noses. Really appreciate the things in your life that do not cost a thing. Free yourself from the illusion that only success and money can bring you happiness, and realize that happiness is all around you if you just open your eyes to it.

CHAPTER 15

Twenty-First Century Ills

I recently read a very interesting article by Glenn Fisher in *Creating Wealth* that seemed to say it all:

- The fact that the mainstream media is set up to instil a sense of jealousy and resentment in us all (and not just the news, I'm talking about TV entertainment too).
- The fact that the vast majority of our politicians have been forced into self-serving isolation, and any open-minded honesty is likely to be met with derision or hostility.
- And the fact that the dawn of 24-hour social media means you have a live running reminder that while you're stuck earning money for your family, someone else is out having fun.

They all lead to you thinking negatively. They lead to you being stressed out. They lead to you feeling depressed.[36]

---

36   Glenn Fisher, "How to Live a Happy Life in the Angry 21st Century—Part Two," *Creating Wealth*, Medium, August 4, 2016, https://medium.com/@creatingwealth/how-to-live-a-happy-life-in-the-angry-21st-century-part-two-c8cab2cf794d.

STOP THINKING NEGATIVELY

The amazing thing is that even if nothing good is happening for you in the moment, just thinking about pleasurable things from your past can release the happiness hormone serotonin, instantly lifting your mood and making you feel better.

I love to collect things from my travels, and my home is full of things that remind me of the great times I've had in far-flung places. I notice, though, that if I'm feeling down, all I have to do is look at one of them, and the memory of a happy time comes flooding back—or even a memory of the moment that I bought the souvenir. My immediate worries, or the cause of my depression, will be forgotten for a moment—and even that moment helps. What I've noticed is that it is no good trying to create happy serotonin-producing moments while you are still held captive by negative thoughts. I realized some time ago that a lot of things that bothered me and led me to negative thought territory came from social media, so I decided to ration my exposure to it. I stopped watching predictable, negative, and rubbish TV that had no value to it and instead watched documentaries on nature and travel. It was like someone had had a declutter in my brain; I immediately felt better and less edgy and confused.

If you allow negative thoughts and negativity to surround you and take hold, you will eventually drown in an unpleasant soup of all that is horrible in your life. You might find it fun to play computer games from morning until night, or watch pornography, but make no mistake that everything will eventually take its toll on you. You may have heard the saying "rubbish in, rubbish out." Is that what you really want for your brain?

DITCH THE STRESS

I know you're probably sick of hearing it—that you should simply stop getting so stressed. But it's not that easy, right? Using the power of your mind to avoid getting stressed is not that easy, but suffering from a suppression of serotonin caused by stress is no picnic either. I'm sure you've heard people say that there is good and bad stress and that they thrive on being stressed and put under pressure. Unfortunately, this is not true. Stress is just bad. Anyone who says they thrive on stress is actually just thriving on being able to control the stress they feel. And that is a very good thing, of course. The good feeling they get is actually due to dopamine release. Dopamine is quite similar to serotonin and will give you a feeling of well-being when you have achieved something.

In his article, Glen Fisher mentions "the horrible and the miserable." The quote, he says, comes from one of Woody Allen's most famous films, *Annie Hall*. In it, Woody explains his very pessimistic view of life to the lead actress, Diane Keaton. Fisher explains, "There are two kinds of people, the horrible and the miserable. The horrible are terminal cases, people with no hope. The miserable, he says, are everyone else."[37] He observed, "The punch line has a quirky positivity to it: when you go through life, you should be thankful that you're miserable."[38]

Maybe that is the reason that people like to watch soap operas like EastEnders and *Coronation Street*, Fisher supposes, which usually deal with horrible problems and miserable situations that people find themselves in. As

---

37 Fisher, "How to Live a Happy Life."
38 Fisher, "How to Live a Happy Life."

another crisis hits our favorite soap and yet more people end up in hospital or worse, do we really need the negativity it all brings to drag us down? I don't think so. Exposing yourself to this sort of thing is not good and will do nothing for your positivity and your drive to go forward and make a success of your life. You may think that when you turn the television off or shut down the phone or computer for the night, all that you've been exposed to goes with it. The truth is, it doesn't; it just adds another layer of misery to pull you down, and you don't need that.

Your exposure to all the tech you rely on and the media that you're glued to is wasting your precious time—time you could be using to improve your life and your prospects and be better for yourself and for other people. But as well as that, allowing your mind to be polluted with all this rubbish will have a biological effect on your ability to have the happy life you are looking for.

CHAPTER 16

What Is the Answer?

We are guilty of watching too much TV, spending too much time on social media, and being overly influenced by what we see in the press, in advertisements, and in the endless articles about the impossibly rich and beautiful people we know we will never be. I get my strength and happiness from what I believe in. Whatever we believe or don't believe, we all have the right to feel happy in our lives.

I can remember my grandmother telling me that, when she was a child, she would get a penny and an orange for Christmas and be absolutely delighted. Compare that with today's children's expectations and the huge piles of presents that seem to be obligatory no matter the financial position of the parents. Every year, without fail, we hear stories of how people get into serious debt catering to their children's every desire at Christmas. And it's not just because these children are greedy or spoiled and their demands are ever more difficult to satisfy. In their own world, our children are under as much pressure as we are as adults, judged for the labels they wear and the phones that they carry almost before anyone considers what kind of people they are.

A whole generation will grow up feeling that the only way they will be valued or liked is through conforming to what they should look like, what phone they should have, what people they should hang around with, and even what TV shows they should watch. Wouldn't this make for happiness? I really don't think so.

It sounds an impossible idea with today's overwhelming reliance on technology to imagine going back to simpler pleasures and pastimes that might make us happier. I recently read about a young lad who was so addicted to playing on his Xbox that he actually caused himself physical harm. So determined was he to keep playing that he would delay going to the toilet, and over time this led to his bowel becoming severely distorted. He was treated for his addiction but also had to have surgery.[39]

Another program that has been on television recently, called *Planet Child*, a 2019 documentary produced by Christin Collerton and starring Chris van Tuleken, Xand van Tulleken, and Chloe Solomen, shows how children in different parts of the world respond to various things.[40] What struck me in this program was that some children taking part were from the Himba tribe, an indigenous people with an estimated population of about fifty thousand who live in northern Namibia, in the Kunene Region (formerly Kaokoland) and on the other side of the Kunene River in Angola. These children had no tech and spent their days

---

39 Tom Davidson, "Boy, 10, Needed Bowel Surgery After He Stopped Going to the Toilet During Eight-Hour World of Warcraft Binges," *Mirror*, June 21, 2018, https://www.mirror.co.uk/news/uk-news/boy-10-needed-bowel-surgery-12757105.

40 Christian Collerton, director, *Planet Child*, episode 1, (United Kingdom: The Garden, 2019).

learning how to hunt and care for animals or prepare food for the rest of the tribe. Children would have lived this way a couple of centuries ago in the West. Childhood would've been cut short, and as soon as they were able, like the Himba children, they would have been set to work. We consider ourselves to have advanced from those dark days of child labor. But what do we have in their place? The children of the Himba tribe looked happy and carefree despite their responsibilities. The children of the West in the twenty-first century are committing suicide after being bullied on social media, gaining so much weight that predictions are that their parents will outlive them, or getting treatment for addiction to social media or gaming. How can we expect a child whose early life has been blighted by these twenty-first-century ills to grow into a happy adult? We can't.

We all want to be happy, but how are we going to achieve that? Glenn Fisher's article would be a good place to start. We need to look carefully at what we're doing—and, even if it makes us unpopular with our children, we need to be brave enough to shield them from what can hurt them.

CHAPTER 17

Free Yourself

Nelson Mandela spent twenty-seven years in prison, and most of those years were spent in isolation on Robben Island, off the coast of Cape Town, South Africa.

Any encounters he had with visitors from the outside world were very short and very strictly controlled. Mandela had no confidence that he would ever emerge alive from his captivity.

An article I read with fascination last year in the *Washington Post* really made me think.[41]

The article's writer, Siobhán O'Grady, presented a new collection of letters Mandela had written from prison, showing us how the freedom fighter who would eventually become South Africa's first Black president kept himself grounded and connected to the outside world, even as apartheid leaders tried everything they could to silence him.

---

41 Siobhán O'Grady, "How Did Nelson Mandela Survive 27 Years in Prison? A New Collection of Letters Sheds Light," *Washington Post*, July 18, 2018, https://www.washingtonpost.com/news/worldviews/wp/2018/07/18/how-did-nelson-mandela-survive-27-years-in-prison-a-new-collection-of-letters-sheds-light/.

The Prison Letters of Nelson Mandela, edited by South African journalist Sahm Venter, featured 255 letters from Mandela—about half of which had never been seen publicly before. O'Grady tells us that Venter, who spent nearly a decade reviewing Mandela's letters, said in an email to the *Washington Post* that the wisdom Mandela displayed in his letters is "particularly relevant in the world today, which is experiencing the rise of...racism, sexism, and xenophobia."

The book shows us the personal side of South Africa's most famous man, something that Mandela was perhaps a bit reluctant to share publicly after he had been jailed and before the publication of his memoir, *Long Walk to Freedom.*

Stop and imagine for a minute what you would feel like if you were imprisoned and had no idea when or if you would ever be released.

While he was being kept in prison, Mandela says that one thing he missed very desperately was being able to raise his children. He also wrote about the torment he felt over being unable to bury either his mother or his oldest son, Thembi. His son died in 1969 in a car accident.

His writing tells of the supreme effort he made to try to humanize himself to the prison officials in charge of him before asking them for special permission to attend family funerals. His approach, however, did not work, and every request was denied. This shows just a glimpse of the pain that Nelson Mandela must have felt as he languished in prison and grieved for those he loved and who he could not even say goodbye to.

"The feeling of anguish & depression that had hit me so viciously when I received the horrible news of his death returned and began to gnaw away mercilessly at my insides," he wrote to his wife, Winnie, after he had a visit from Thoko Mandela, his son Thembi's young widow.[42]

How on earth did he keep his chin up, keep from going mad in the midst of all this sorrow and disappointment? How would you? How would I?

I have always believed that even if you are physically imprisoned, your soul can be free—but how do we achieve that? An article written by Michael Annese in *SUCCESS* titled "How to Break Free and Really Live" discusses this belief.[43]

Do you sometimes feel as though you are stuck in a rut, on the endless hamster wheel that has become your everyday routine? Many of us, without even realizing it, can become mired in the mundane and the routine. But there is a way to break out. It will not be easy, but it can be done.

To start with, you need to stop making excuses for yourself and putting things off until next week, next month, or next year. Making the break and making a change means actually getting on with it and not prevaricating anymore.

Here are some starters that will get you well on your way.

1. Leave the past where it belongs in the past. Draw a line under past failures, and leave them behind you as you move in a more positive direction. Learn lessons from whatever didn't go well, and consolidate on whatever did go well.
2. Next, pose these questions to yourself:
    A. What is my purpose in life?
    B. What do I do really well?

---

[42] O'Grady, "How Did Nelson Mandela Survive 27 Years in Prison?"

[43] Michael Annese, "How to Break Free and Really Live," *SUCCESS*, January 24, 2017, https://www.success.com/how-to-break-free-and-really-live/.

c. What things do I love to do the most?
3. Keep your eyes on the prize. You have only one life in which to make an impact and to follow the dreams that you have. Whatever you feel you should be doing, however unattainable that might be, don't ignore it because it is possible. You may be able to modify your dreams slightly to attain a better way of life for yourself
4. Always be a leader and not a follower because it is only by leading that you can go in the direction that you want to go. If you follow, you give away that choice.
5. Always have an inquiring mind. The adage says that knowledge is power, and that is very true.

Use the answers to your questions to give yourself a new plan of what you can do to make your dreams and aspirations a reality.

CHAPTER 18

Aim High

I want to ask now: what if you really are held not by invisible chains but by prison bars like Nelson Mandela was? How do you put into practice the great advice that Michael Annese gives in his article? It would be very difficult indeed—and even more difficult not to give up and count the situation and yourself as a hopeless case.

Even with great faith, it can be tricky to keep your head above water when everything around you seems to be going wrong.

In the *Washington Post* article, O'Grady discusses the heartbreaking details of the letter that Mandela wrote to his children. It was the only fathering that he could practically do.[44]

The letter shows that Mandela tried his very best to be an influence and a support as a father even if it had to be from prison. While his daughters were young at the time that he was arrested, Mandela met his family's difficulties

---
44   O'Grady, "How Did Nelson Mandela Survive 27 Years in Prison?"

head on and did not shy away from telling his girls where he was and what his being in prison meant.

Other letters he wrote to family members and family friends show clearly how concerned he was about how the children were getting on, especially when their mother, Winnie, was arrested in 1969.

That year, Mandela wrote to his daughters and said plainly that they would now have to do without the comforts they would always have had from their mother. He wrote, "For long you may live like orphans." The letter also gave us an insight into the deep agony he felt about Winnie's arrest and revealed that he was ready and willing to share the pain with his young children. In another letter, Mandela wrote, "My heart bleeds as I think of her sitting in some police cell far away from home, perhaps alone and without anybody to talk to, and with nothing to read." This is real pain.[45]

Another article I saw as I researched for this book was one that made me think about this and about how we often put ourselves in our own solitary confinement, and I decided to read on to see what I could learn.

> The effect of solitary confinement on mental health can be devastating—what techniques can kidnap victims, hostages, and prisoners use to get through the ordeal?

> "No one knows that you are there, so you are nothing. You are zero."

> For many months, Tabir was kept in solitary confinement in a cell in North Africa, imprisoned for his political views. His

---

45 O'Grady, "How Did Nelson Mandela Survive 27 Years in Prison?"

room didn't have a bed or a toilet. The sole feature was a small, high window which let a wan light through.

He recalls the countless, long days passing in complete silence. But then after sunset, and stretching through till dawn, he could hear the wailing of fellow prisoners being tortured—a sound that provided some comfort, since it was a confirmation that he was still alive in a world shared with other people.[46]

The article mentions Pelican Bay State Prison, one of the toughest in the US, housing more than a thousand prisoners in solitary confinement. Prisoners do not have access to rehabilitation programs and are separated by glass screens from visiting relatives and lawyers. Their ninety-minute break takes place in a concrete cell with twenty-foot-high (six meters) walls and a meshed plastic roof.

According to Amnesty International, in 2011, more than five hundred prisoners in California had spent more than a decade in solitary, and seventy-eight had spent more than two decades.[47]

Craig Haney believes that solitary confinement devastates some prisoners so much that the practice amounts to torture.

> "Some people have an immediate, profoundly negative reaction to it," says Craig Haney, a professor of psychology at the

---

[46] William Kremer and Claudia Hammond, "How Do People Survive Solitary Confinement?," BBC News, June 13, 2013, https://www.bbc.com/news/magazine-22878268.

[47] "USA: California Authorities Urged to End Shocking Conditions in Prison Isolation Units," Amnesty International, September 27, 2012, https://www.amnesty.org/en/latest/news/2012/09/usa-california-authorities-urged-end-shocking-conditions-prison-isolation-units/.

University of California, Santa Cruz, who has studied the impact of solitary confinement on the inmates of Pelican Bay.

"For some people, there is something terrifying about being placed in an environment where you are completely alone, isolated from others and where you cannot connect to other people."

Those inmates not affected by this "isolation panic" may still slip into long-term depression and hopelessness. Then the environment takes its toll on cognitive ability, as the prisoners' intellectual skills begin to decay. They may suffer lapses in memory. At the most extreme, prisoners could even undergo a complete breakdown.[48]

---

48 Kremer and Hammond, "How Do People Survive Solitary Confinement?"

CHAPTER 19

Set Your Soul Free

In the BBC article published in June 2013 written by William Kremer and Claudia Hammond of the BBC World Service "How Do People Survive Solitary Confinement?" David Alexander, a psychiatrist and trauma expert who contributed to the article, said that very often hostages can be kept in conditions similar to solitary confinement, without toilets or washing facilities. His advice for that is simple.[49]

"If it's filthy, then set about cleaning it," says Alexander. Start to scrape the mess to one side of the cell.

He tells how, with one corner dedicated for peeing, you want to be sure that the pee will run downward. He also recommended making a section for a "living area" in the cell that is kept as neat and tidy as possible and that, however difficult, prisoners should try to keep as clean they can. He goes further and suggests cleaning one's fingernails using the nails on the opposite hand, and if nails become broken or rough, filing them against the wall. These little

---

49   Kremer and Hammond, "How Do People Survive Solitary Confinement?"

acts of keeping tidy will help someone retain a feeling of identity—part psychological and part physical.

Communication is also something that must be taken seriously, Alexander says. Of course, there may be periods with no chance of communication that will result in completely losing touch with the world outside and may even start a prisoner wondering whether, indeed, they even still exist.

In the article, Tabir, who was imprisoned in North Africa, tells of how he spent his nights singing or even talking to himself so that he could regain a feeling of his own physical presence. When he was most desperate for contact, however negative, he would pick fights with the guards who were looking after him. In America, this type of behavior is called "cell extraction." What it means is that the inmate will not go along with the orders he has been given, maybe by refusing to allow the dishes from his meal to be cleared away. This behavior will lead to guards arriving at the cell to restrain him forcibly. It is the stuff of nightmares for most of us, but for people like Tabir, it was at least human contact, in some form.

Alexander goes on to say that if someone is being held hostage, a personal routine is key. For this, Alexander recommends getting into a routine similar to the one that may have existed at home. A hostage should do anything possible to impose structure and order in their world. This, he says, will help with a feeling of identity and will also help mount a defense against what those keeping you hostage want for you.[50]

What any captive wants as an ideal outcome is for a pris-

---

[50] Kremer and Hammond, "How Do People Survive Solitary Confinement?"

oner to become a victim of "learned helplessness," a state in which they are convinced that anything that they try to do will be a failure.

In Eastern Europe, hostage Andre was held as a political prisoner for many months in solitary confinement. During that time, he experienced several moments of hope that were cruelly dashed. He would be told that he was being released only to find that all that was happening was he was being moved to another prison. Another tactic his captors used to wear him down was repeated searches, often eight times each day. Andre says that he had to teach himself to avoid going to any extreme. He felt the only way to survive was to stay on an even keel. Andre was successful in managing his emotions, and he was able to read for many hours, which kept him busy. He also constructed haiku poems and might spend a whole day trying to pinpoint what three lines would most ideally record a feeling or a memory.

Then came the day when he was actually released. Because he had trained himself to avoid extremes of emotion, Andre barely showed any reaction.[51]

Alexander says that a lot of prisoners who have been in solitary confinement find it extremely difficult, even when they are released, to escape the feeling of being emotionally numb. This may have the long-term effect of making it difficult for them to trust partners or friends or to form meaningful relationships. PTSD (post-traumatic stress disorder) is another common after-effect—as are anxiety, sleeplessness, depression, flashbacks, and a sensitivity to loud noise.[52]

---

[51] Kremer and Hammond, "How Do People Survive Solitary Confinement?"

[52] Kremer and Hammond, "How Do People Survive Solitary Confinement?"

We can all learn a lot from such an experience. Although most of us will not be in a physical prison or be held hostage, we can make hostages and prisoners of ourselves, getting too wrapped up in the things in life that really are not important.

I hope that, like me, you have enjoyed the inspiration I have found in the works of other people. I hope the words I have written have been something you have wanted to hear too. I think I would like to end this book with the words that Tabir, a true survivor, said:

"Smile and be happy and don't be afraid of anybody."

www.ingramcontent.com/pod-product-compliance
Lightning Source LLC
Chambersburg PA
CBHW031200020426
42333CB00013B/761